Mou

No friends
in high places

THE EDITORIAL CARTOONS OF THEO MOUDAKIS

Pottersfield Press
Lawrencetown Beach, Nova Scotia, Canada

Canadian Cataloguing in Publication Data
Moudakis, Theo.

No friends in high places

ISBN 0-919001-90-4

1. Canadian wit and humour, Pictorial. 2. Canada - Politics and government - Caricatures and cartoons. I. Title.

NC1449.M68A4 1995   971.064'8'0207   C95-950043-X

Back cover photo by Tony Caldwell
Printed and bound in Canada

Published with the financial support of The Canada Council, The Department of Canadian Heritage and The Nova Scotia Department of Education.

Pottersfield Press
RR 2, Lawrencetown Beach
Porters Lake
Nova Scotia B0J 2S0

Acknowledgements

Doug MacKay and Bill Turpin, the editors of my universe, for taking a chance on an inexperienced young ethnic punk; for allowing me not only to learn on the job, but to be risky, bold, inventive, and a little nasty; and for letting me cut a lot of corners while putting this book together;

Joan Fraser, for inadvertently scuttling my plans to become a commercial artist;

Terry Mosher, who I would never dare tell to his face what an absolute honor it is to have the support and encouragement of someone like him;

Frank Myrskog, for help with the cover;

Rob Roberts, for help with that blasted computer;

Judy Kavanagh, for being the closest thing I have to a right-hand man;

Cathy MacDonald, for winning the Name Mou's Book contest;

And Ethel and Nick, for everything else.

Foreword

i used to be the editor-in-chief of *The Daily News* in Halifax. But sometime last year, I became instead the full-time apologist for a Greek cartoonist from Montreal. This is not as bad as it sounds. Theo Moudakis is a good guy to work for.

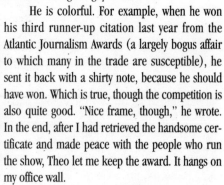

He is colorful. For example, when he won his third runner-up citation last year from the Atlantic Journalism Awards (a largely bogus affair to which many in the trade are susceptible), he sent it back with a shirty note, because he should have won. Which is true, though the competition is also quite good. "Nice frame, though," he wrote. In the end, after I had retrieved the handsome certificate and made peace with the people who run the show, Theo let me keep the award. It hangs on my office wall.

He is paranoid. For example, he's pretty sure any personal attacks against him — and certainly the misdirection of any awards — have something to do with his being Greek and From Away, and very little to do with his own published opinions. This makes him friendly and attentive to the few people he trusts.

He is malicious and won't back down. When one of his recurring characters ventured the opinion last year that the unionists trying to unseat Premier John Savage (OK, *all* unionists) were "disciples of hell," union members from sea to shining sea rose as one to condemn Theo and *The Daily News* for publishing an opinion different from theirs. In response, Theo provoked them further with a false apology, in turn drawing even more mail. This was instructive for all concerned, and gave Theo and me some airtime on local radio and TV. Mostly we learned how fragile freedom of speech might be in certain hands.

He is unreasonably talented. Theo takes his medium and shakes it, expands it, makes it more alive. He uses text (for which he has a satirical gift), he evokes with ease anything from an old Eaton's catalogue to *Mad* magazine to an 18th century nautical chart, and he works very, very, hard at all those little cross-hatched lines. As well, his political antennae (he is in a foreign land, remember) work better every day. Who else could have angered the Curragh Resources board, the Human Rights Commission, the black community, the Greek community, the labor movement, certain tycoons, the civil service, women, and all three political parties, to name but a few?

In the midst of one of the union boycotts last year, a reader wrote offering support (we'd been publishing as much of the critical mail as we could). "Whatever happened to freedom of speech, expression, opinion, ideas?" she asked. "Good grief! I claim to have enough brains to read everything and agree or disagree as I choose. So don't ever change — you make us *think!*"

And so it is with Theo. He makes us laugh, and then we think.

Douglas MacKay

Introduction

Canadians — in general a dull, responsible lot — have produced an overabundance of humorists for some unknown reason.

Many of the best had to go to the U.S., where they started magazines like *National Lampoon* or wrote for TV shows like Saturday Night Live, or began appearing in stand-up comic joints from Bangor to San Diego.

But our cartoonists — recognized as being among the best working anywhere today — have stayed home.

And why?

Because — frankly — we tend to get away with more up here, and have more fun in the process.

As opposed to following the party line of the newspapers that hire us (as our *confreres* in the U.S. usually have to), we are allowed — indeed, often encouraged — to thumb our noses at any and all currently occupying the political spectrum.

Witness Theo Moudakis's recent cartoon shots at labor unions. Theo is hardly a paid propagandist for the right wing, having drawn some monstrously critical cartoons of the Tories.

But when Mou decided to do the same to the left in the form of a tongue-in-cheek comic strip, the howls of righteous indignation from the brothers and sisters were heard from coast to coast.

Hey, unions are neither perfect nor above criticism. And screw 'em if they can't take a joke, eh?

Francis Bacon (not the painter, the other one) once said that saltiness is preferable to bitterness. Therein lies the key to any successful satirist.

Theo Moudakis, drawing his way through such experiences, is rapidly earning his spurs and — in the process — has become one of the best young cartoonists around.

With this, his first book of what I'm sure will be many, permit me to welcome you to his world.

Aislin (Terry Mosher)
The Montreal Gazette

THEO – A GREEK, BEARING THE GIFT

Portraiture

Preston Manning

Kim Campbell and Friend

Jean Chretien and John Savage

13

Paul Martin

THE NDP PLANS
TO MAKE QUITE A
SPLASH
NEXT ELECTION!

Audrey McLaughlin

14

Bill Clinton

Elizabeth Regina II

15

Nelson Mandela

The Nation

Mou's ··· Believe It or Don't!

A BIT OF PALEONTOLOGICAL DETECTIVE WORK WAS PUT TO USE RECENTLY WHEN A PERFECTLY PRESERVED SPECIMEN OF **STEGOSAURUS CANADIANUS** WAS UNEARTHED IN NORTHERN QUEBEC.

A VARIETY OF EVIDENCE, INCLUDING PELVIC-BONE STRUCTURE, FOSSILIZED FOOTPRINTS, AND OLD NEWSPAPERS FOUND UNDERNEATH THE JURASSIC REMAINS, SHOW CONCLUSIVELY THAT CANADIANS HAVE BEEN GRAPPLING UNSUCCESSFULLY WITH THE NATIONAL UNITY QUESTION FOR WELL OVER 65 MILLION YEARS!

**Gun Owners and their logic may be
hazardous to our health.**

24

"Let us love one another:
for love is of God;
and everyone that loveth
is born of God
and knoweth God.
Except, of course,
those icky homosexuals."
-I John 4:7

Small-Time Liberal
Backbencher
Roseanne Skoke

25

27

29

Kim Campbell's **Deficit-Cutting Techniques**

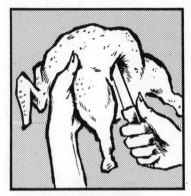

1. Grasp economy firmly and insert Tory Deficit-Cutting Agenda.

2. Using a jabbing motion, administer deep cuts to Transfer Payments, Defence, etc, etc.

3. Gently separate Social Programs from remaining carcass.

4. Quietly carve away at Social Programs, while being extra-careful to deny any such--

5. Oops!

6. Plummet sharply in polls.

33

34

36

EXTRA — THE LEDGER-DISPATCH

WAR OVER
Japan Surrenders Unconditionally

The Press — FINAL

POLIO CONQUERED

5 CENTS — FINAL EDITION — News

MAN ON THE MOON!

The Canada Shopper

BOURASSA DOES LUNCH!

The Charlottetown Accord

39

41

December 6, 1989

44

National Gallery Acquisition:
"No. 16". Oil on Canvas.
$1.8 Million.

National Gallery Acquisition:
"Voice of Fire". Acrylic on Canvas.
$1.8 Million.

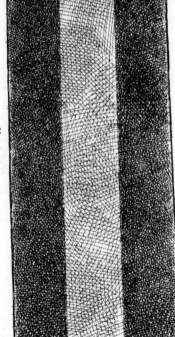

Attention National Gallery.
Available for Immediate Acquisition:
"Untitled". Felt-Tip on Paper.
Call 987-2222, ask for Mou. (Preferably before I go on holidays next week.)

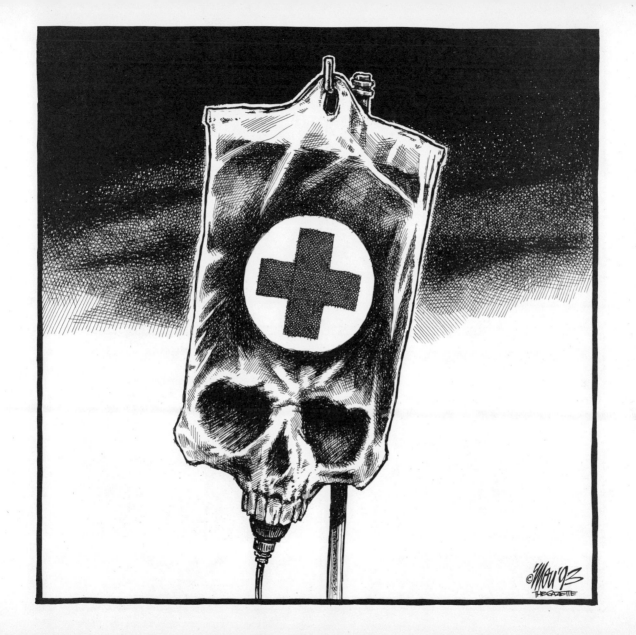

49

☞ THINGS THAT JUST NEVER QUITE CAUGHT ON

1. BETA

2. THE GORBY DOLL

3. FRUIT-FLAVORED POTATO CHIPS

4. AUDREY

50

The Province

An Adventure
15 Years In The Making.

A JOHN SAVAGE FILM

LIBERAL GOV'T

BACKROOM PICTURES PRESENTS A SHADOWY MEN FROM A SHADOWY PARTY PRODUCTION
JOHN SAVAGE IN "LIBERAL GOV'T" WITH MANNING MacPALEOPOLITICS GERRY O'SAURUS ETC ETC
BASED ON THE TURFING OF VINCE MacLEAN SPECIAL VISUAL EFFECTS BY BRISTOL COMMUNICATIONS
ORCHESTRATED BY JOHN YOUNG PRODUCED BY HOW MUR WRITTEN AND DIRECTED BY JOHN SAVAGE
A 'Mou' JOINT

53

54

An Apology.

It has recently come to our attention that the editorial cartoon of August 19, 1994 (pictured above) has been much photocopied and distributed amongst members of Nova Scotia's trade unions, prompting scores of complaints daily to this newspaper, including several cancelled subscriptions, and at least one veiled threat of bodily harm to this cartoonist.

We at The Daily News Cartoon wish to apologize to all for not making clearer the limitations and legalities of cartoon photocopying. The trade unionists' usurping of this cartoon for their own purposes is a clear violation of **The Canada Cartoon Copyright Act** (para. D, sub-para. IV), and **Interpol's Cartoon Piracy Act** (The Hague, 1987).

Unless the perpetrators of these serious crimes wish to feel the full sting of the law, **we at The Daily News Cartoon shall expect to receive full payment** for no less than **all** lost royalties, **all** lost sales revenues (including interest), as well as **full** compensation resulting from any undue mental anguish herein, thereof, et cetera.

Make all cheques (**no post-dates please!**) payable to:
Mou, c/o The Daily News
P.O. Box 8330, Station A
Halifax NS, B3K 5M1

56

57

Alexa McDonough
Steps Down As
NDP Leader

Consumer Affairs
Minister Guy Brown

61

Ottawa's **Fishery Aid** Techniques

A. After imposing Northern Cod Moratorium, administer limited CPR (Compensation Program for Recovery) to Fishery.

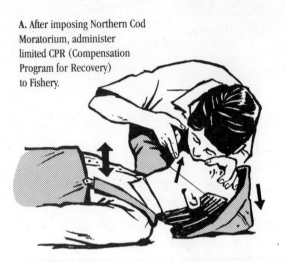

B. Quickly dispense with compensation and attempt to revive Fishery by offering "Educational Upgrading".

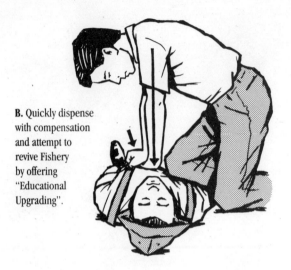

C. If still unsuccessful, present generous retraining programs while delivering devastating blows to remaining Fishery.

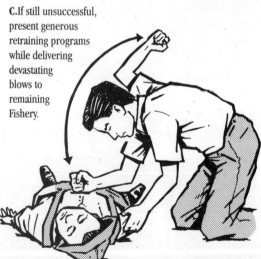

D. Leave Pittance.

Mou's --- Believe It or Don't!

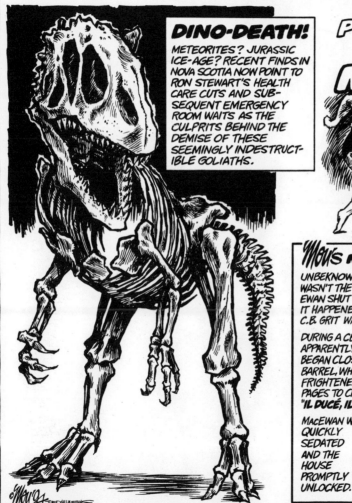

DINO-DEATH!

METEORITES? JURASSIC ICE-AGE? RECENT FINDS IN NOVA SCOTIA NOW POINT TO RON STEWART'S HEALTH CARE CUTS AND SUBSEQUENT EMERGENCY ROOM WAITS AS THE CULPRITS BEHIND THE DEMISE OF THESE SEEMINGLY INDESTRUCTIBLE GOLIATHS.

PUBLIC SECTOR UNIONS: MYTH...

...AND REALITY

Mou's NOVA SCOTIA FUN-FACT

UNBEKNOWNST TO MANY, APRIL 29 1994 WASN'T THE **FIRST** TIME SPEAKER PAUL MacEWAN SHUT DOWN PROVINCE HOUSE. IT HAPPENED ON JUNE 28 1993, THE DAY THE C.B. GRIT WAS ELECTED TO THE SPEAKER'S CHAIR.

DURING A CELEBRATION THAT EVENING, MATTERS APPARENTLY GOT OUT OF HAND AND MacEWAN BEGAN CLOSING UP THE HOUSE, LOCK STOCK AND BARREL, WHILE FORCING FRIGHTENED YOUNG PAGES TO CHANT **"IL DUCÉ, IL DUCÉ!"**

MacEWAN WAS QUICKLY SEDATED AND THE HOUSE PROMPTLY UNLOCKED.

Finance Minister
Bernie Boudreau

G-7 Meeting
is Announced
for Moira
Ducharme's
Halifax

The Nova Scotia Election Campaign

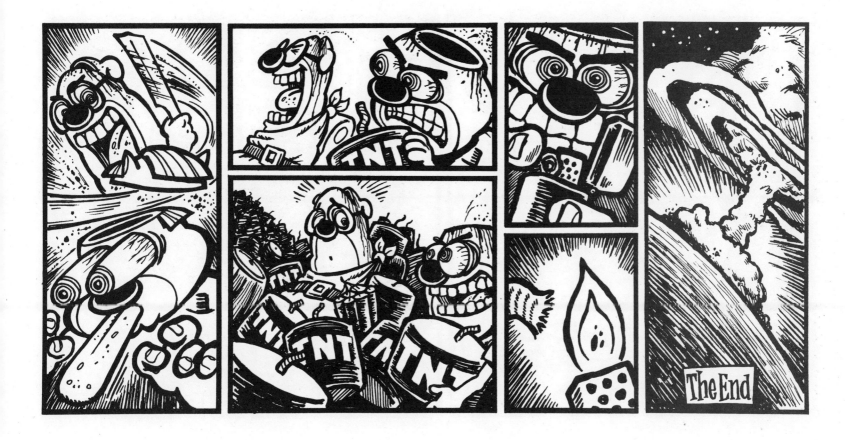

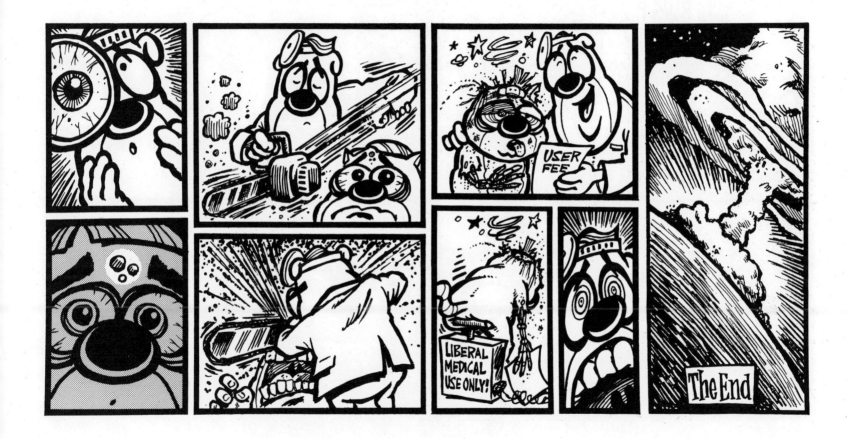

On-Duty Dartmouth
Cop Shoots Deer

Dartmouth Mayor
Gloria McCluskey and
One of her Finest

Nova Scotia's **Winter Olympics '94**

Morning Car Removal
Super-Endurance

Slippery Sidewalk
Giant Slalom Classic

Pothole Swerve & Pedestrian
Side-Swipe Biathlon

Wind Chill/ Frost-Bite/ Gangrene
Combined

Hypothermic Homeless Person
Freestyle Snub

TV Weatherman Payback
Dream Event

Synchronized
Seasonal Depression

Synchronized Seasonal
Anti-Depressant Indulgence

The February
Travel Agency Sprint

Atlantic Canada
Opportunities
Agency (ACOA)
Continues to
Fund Dubious
Business
Ventures

ANCIENT RUINS... IN GREECE

...IN EGYPT

...ROME

...THE MARITIMES

The Evolution of **Brain Size & Function**

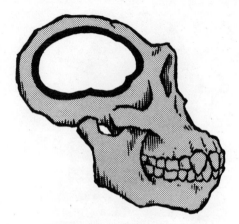

Australopithecus

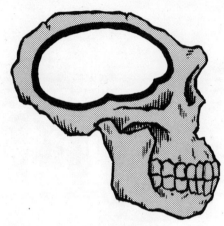

Neanderthal Man

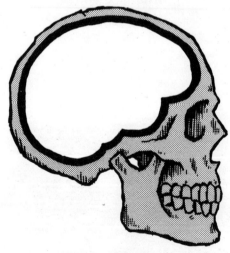

Homo Sapien

Halifax Council

If Dr. Savage says it's OK, then it must be good for you!

Now everyone, from the lad who delivers your Daily News to the senior barely able to make ends meet, can enjoy the warm comforts of tobacco smoking thanks to Dr. Savage Brand Affordable Cigarettes. Dangers? As you can see, the pluses far out-wiegh the minuses!

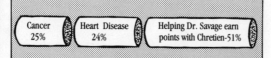

| Cancer 25% | Heart Disease 24% | Helping Dr. Savage earn points with Chretien-51% |

You'll look plenty smart around the schoolyard now that Dr. Savage Brand Affordable Cigarettes are within your financial reach.

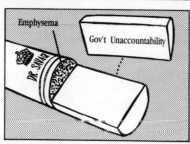

And you'll be pleased to know that you and your new-found pastime will be directly participating in the wiping out of this awful illegal cigarette trade that is crippling our province.

Percentage of Illegal Trade in Nova Scotia

Dr. Savage, you make it all better.

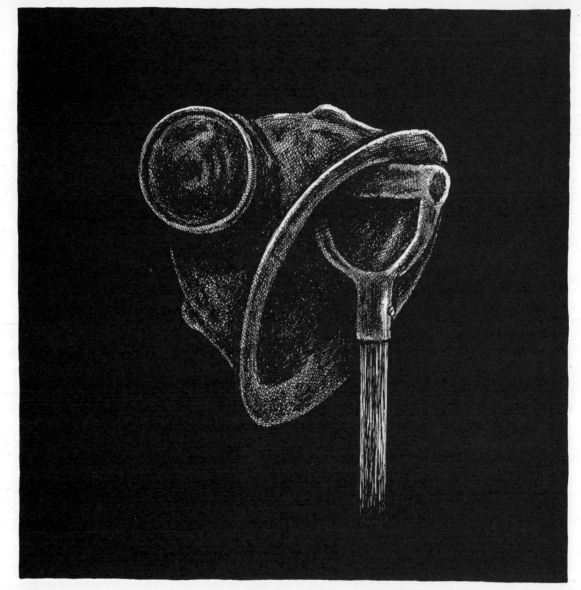

*Westray Disaster
Kills 26 Miners*

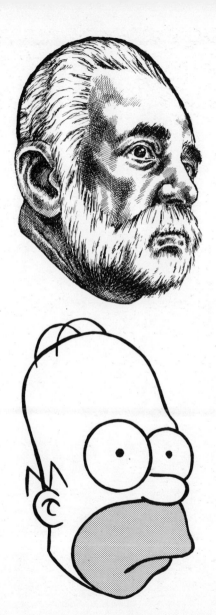

Leroy Legere,
Then-Minister
in Charge of
Safety in
the Mines

*Public Prosecutor
John Pearson
Forever Unable
to Lay Charges
Against Westray
Mine Owners*

88

What *exactly* constitutes making "insults to, or assaults or libels upon" the Speaker of the House?

This?

This?

This?

This?

Speaker of the House Threatens Journalist with Jail Time over Criticisms

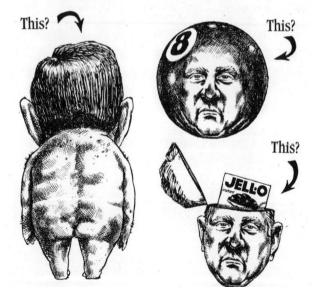

JELL-O

This?

All of the above. Which is why we at The Daily News Cartoon are offering this as a public service to other cartoonists on how NOT to draw Paul MacEwan. So, remember: Don't be fools... Heed the rules!

This?...Most definitely.

The World

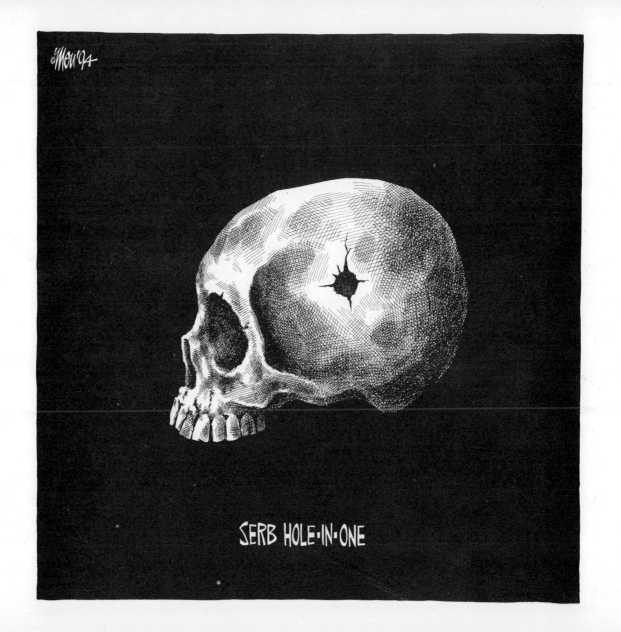

SERB HOLE·IN·ONE

97

100

Bosnia

Miscellaneous

Unpublished

Essential Accessories for this Season

The Crocheted Cap

Foulard by Boss

Fringed Beret with Fur-Lined Stole

Prozac

(Only 55 Shopping Days Left)

Cartoonist Banned From Annual Greek-Fest

Terry Donahoe

John Savage

Donald Cameron

Rollie Thornhill

A slithery solution?

By PETER HAYS
The Daily News

Mary Appelhof has worms for sale that eat just about anything and turns it into rich, odorless compost. Just place her patented "Worm-a-way" under the kitchen sink, add some worms and start composting.

"It's a pretty weird thing, to do composting in your own home", Appelhof admits. "But when people start thinking about having toxic...

OH, HELEN, OUR NEW **WORM-A-WAY**® HOME COMPOST IS A **DREAM**!! AND JUST A FEW MINUTES A DAY UNDER THE SINK HAS TURNED OUR TIMMY INTO AN ABSOLUTE **TREASURE** OF OBEDIENCE!

Unpublished

114

Dartmouth Cop

Vince MacLean

Tonya Harding

Ross Bragg

Character From "For Better or Worse" Reveals His Alternative Lifestyle

In response to the personal concerns of Dartmouth Police Chief Don MacRae, We at The Daily News Cartoon proudly announce our new policy of "Image-Positive" Dartmouth Police caricatures.

Wherever possible, We at The Daily News Cartoon shall portray the Dartmouth police officer in nothing but the finest of lights, the most noblest of manners.

We hope our new cartoon policy will go a long way in repairing the obvious damage We at The Daily News Cartoon have so thoughtlessly inflicted on the Dartmouth Police Force and that this policy marks the beginning of a more harmonious---

Ah, who are we kidding.

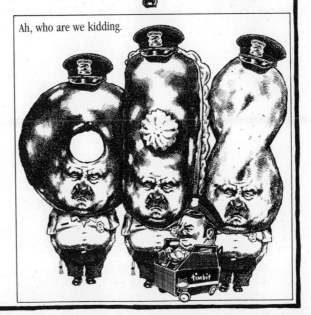

Unpublished

119

"For Pete's sake, Jones,
just get on with it."

"So, Bellows, I hear you really
blew the Ditcorp account."

"You were always very loyal, Pushkin.
How about getting me a coffee
before you leave."

"Dibsies on the Blimpco account."

"He never did know how to relax."

"Now you know, Burnbaum.
Money *does* buy everything."

"It's unanimous, Jenkins.
Possession of a crude nuclear
device automatically clinches you
the lucrative Ditcorp account."

"The old days really are gone
forever, aren't they."

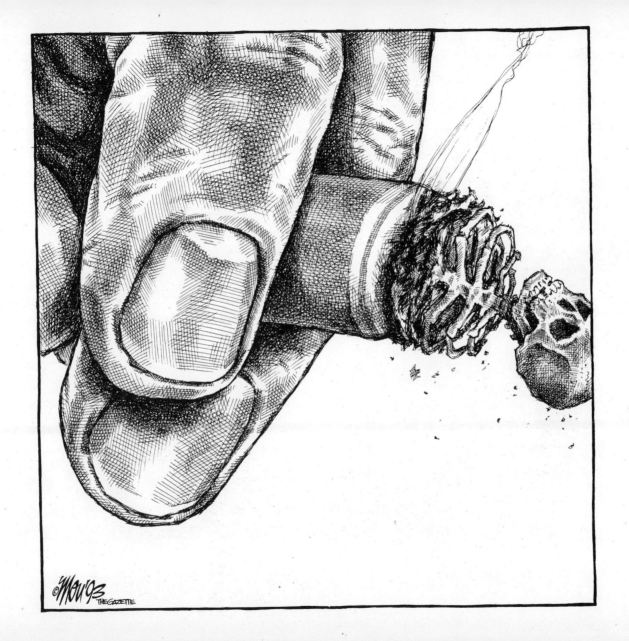

124

Economically Challenged.

HONEY, I THE KID

Unpublished